Praise for REVOLUTIONARY OPTIMISM
7 STEPS FOR LIVING AS A LOVE-ACTIVIST

"*Revolutionary Optimism: 7 Steps for Living as a Love-Activist* is a sacred storehouse of wisdom destined to serve all of us on our journeys. As torchbearers of love seeking illumination, we can draw upon the insights and principles of this book, discovering an indispensable roadmap for personal and global liberation: a clear, step-by-step guide—a timely remedy for the challenges confronting our world."
—Congresswoman Barbara Lee, U.S. House of Representatives

"*Revolutionary Optimism* is a comprehensive and insightful approach to the kind of social change leadership so needed at this time. It offers inspiration as well as practical tools for how to live and lead by 'being the change we want to see happen in the world.'"
—Robert Gass, cofounder, Rockwood Leadership Institute

"So many of us are suffering with a sense of powerlessness, despair, cynicism, and hopelessness about our world. By placing Love at the Center, Dr. Zeitz boldly guides us onto a path of healing into wholeness. He shows us that by tapping into the wellspring of love, we can be nurtured, healed, inspired, and empowered. *Revolutionary Optimism* is exactly the medicine that we need right now, showing us the practical yet profound way forward into a new world where compassion and justice reign, where the deepest yearnings of our collective heart can be realized."
—*Rabbi Shefa Gold, author of* Are We there Yet? Travel as a Spiritual Practice

"*Revolutionary Optimism* is essential in providing a pathway for all activists. It bids us to a higher calling, no matter what cause we are fighting to change, it can only be done holistically and with love for self and others. All humans are interconnected, therefore all causes are; only when we unify, can we change the world. Thank you, Paul, for reminding us of our higher calling—above all else, love your neighbor as yourself."
—Dr. Tabitha Mpamira, founder, Mutura Global Healing

"My life revolves around asking people, 'What makes you optimistic?' *Revolutionary Optimism* by Dr. Paul Zeitz embodies this quest, spotlighting the urgent need for beacons of optimism through the zeitgeist of pessimism and fear. Successful transformative change demands infectiously optimistic leadership. Cultivating the great leader's magnetic optimism starts with simple yet powerful acts: a genuine smile, a warm hello, and a boundless curiosity in others. These seemingly small gestures pave the way for a revolution rooted in love, positivity, deep connection, and collaborative action."
—*Victor Perton, chief optimism officer, The Centre for Optimism,
and author of* Optimism: The How and Why

"*Revolutionary Optimism* is at once timely and robust. As division and polarization seem everywhere, *Revolutionary Optimism* shines a light toward a shared vision of inclusivity and equity for all.

—*Dr. Marcus Anthony Hunter,*
author of Radical Reparations: Healing the Soul of a Nation

"*Revolutionary Optimism* is an amazing book. It gives hope and offers vision. It provides compelling stories of people, including Dr. Zeitz himself, coping with great difficulties and taking small steps every day to build a healthier, better world. Well written and profound. Don't walk, run and get your copy. It can change your life."

—*Sheila Rubin and Bret Lyon, codirectors of the Center*
of the Healing Shame and coauthors of Embracing Shame

"*Revolutionary Optimism* is a powerful reminder that when we put love at the center, all things are possible.

—*Daniela Ligiero, CEO, Together for Girls,*
and cofounder of the Brave Movement

"*Revolutionary Optimism* is the book I have longed to read during these truly polarizing times. This book has shown me how to step in and address the injustices we face today—to see how every person and their actions matter. I now understand the mechanics of how peaceful political action makes a difference. Dr. Paul is right—keeping love at the center of all we do is now more important than ever."

—*Kristine Carlson, coauthor of* Don't Sweat the Small Stuff *books*

"Dr. Paul Zeitz offers a deeply personal and inspiring blueprint around how we can embrace and further live out a commitment to Revolutionary Optimism. With great vulnerability and deep insight, Paul draws upon his own journey as a physician, public health expert, and longtime human rights and peace activist to share practical wisdom on how we can pursue both personal and societal transformation that then transforms our communities and the world."

—*Reverend Adam Russell Taylor, president, Sojourners and author of*
A More Perfect Union: A New Vision for Building the Beloved Community

Revolutionary Optimism

7 Steps for Living as a Love-Centered Activist

Journal & Workbook

ALSO BY DR. PAUL ZEITZ

Waging Justice: A Doctor's Journey to Speak Truth and Be Bold
Waging Optimism: Ushering in a New Era of Justice
Revolutionary Optimism: 7 Steps for Living as a Love-Centered Activist

Revolutionary Optimism

7 Steps for Living as a Love-Centered Activist

Journal & Workbook

DR. PAUL ZEITZ

#unify Movements

Copyright © 2024 by Dr. Paul Zeitz

Published by #unify Movements.

All rights reserved under International and Pan-American Copyright Conventions. No part of this publication may be reproduced, stored in or introduced into a retrieval system, or transmitted in any form or by any means (electronic, mechanical, photocopying, recording or otherwise) without the prior written permission of the publisher. This book is sold subject to the condition that it shall not, by way of trade or otherwise, be lent, resold, hired out, or otherwise circulated without the publisher's prior written consent in any form of binding, cover, or condition other than that in which it was published.

The author of this book does not dispense medical advice or prescribe the use of any technique as a form of treatment for physical, emotional, or medical problems without the advice of a physician, either directly or indirectly. The intent of the author is only to offer information of a general nature to help you in your quest for emotional and spiritual well-being. In the event you use any of the information in this book, which is your constitutional right, the author and publisher assume no responsibility for your actions.

This book is a work of non-fiction. Unless otherwise noted, the author and the publisher make no explicit guarantees as to the accuracy of the information contained in the book and in some cases, the stories, names of people and places have been altered to protect their privacy. Generative AI was not used in the writing of this book. The contents of this book are based solely on the author's knowledge, research, and personal experience.

First Edition

ISBN: 979-8-9902643-3-5 (paperback)
ISBN: 979-8-9902643-2-8 (ebook)

Manufactured in U.S.A.
Book Cover Design | Chelsea Hamre
Internal Design | Alex Lubertozzi
Author Portrait Photography | Sue Dorfman
Editorial Support | Nicholas Tippins and Alex Lubertozzi

*For all our ancestors, for all of us,
for my grandchildren, Sunny Zion Zeitz and Birdie Lou Zeitz,
and for all future generations and all life*

Contents

Introduction 1

Step 1: It's Go Time 7
Rx #1: How Can I Serve Today? 8
Rx #2: Making Commitments 12
Rx #3: Imagining Future Generations 16

Step 2: Self-Liberation 23
Rx #4: Finding Your Soul's Deployment 24
Rx #5: In the Event of a Trigger: Respond with Love 28

Step 3: Accessing Unify Consciousness 35
Rx #6: Breathe to Connect 36
Rx #7: Chanting Praise 40
Rx #8: Silly Sneeze Practice 44

Step 4: Peace-Crafting 51
Rx #9: WAIT: Why Am I Talking? 53
Rx #10: Having Courageous Conversations 57
Rx #11: Practicing Love Speech 61
Rx #12: Trust-O-Meter 65

Step 5: Imagineering 71
Rx #13: Radical Imagination 72
Rx #14: What Are My Visions? 76
Rx #15: Engaging Fear 80
Rx #16: Finding Your Role 84

Step 6: Sparking Peaceful Revolutions 91
Rx #17: Serve as Prophetic Witness 92
Rx #18: Self-Care Tips 96
Rx #19: Failing Forward 100

Step 7: Unifying 107
Rx #20: Looking for Unifying Opportunities 108
Rx #21: Unify Your Vision and Action 112
Rx #22: Death Awareness Practice 116
Rx #23: Self-Commitment to Living as Love-Centered Activist . 120

Journey Onward 125
Acknowledgments 127
About the Author 129

Introduction

IN THE BOOK *Revolutionary Optimism: 7 Steps for Living as a Love-Centered Activist*, I laid out seven steps that anyone can use to go from hopelessness and despair to living your life fully empowered to serve in your highest capacity. Revolutionary Optimism is a healing prescription of action steps, tools, and practices for awakening your political imagination, your bravery, and unifying with others to achieve transformations that up until now may have seemed unattainable.

In practice, Revolutionary Optimism is what it looks like if we work to put love at the center of our own lives and in the center of all our social, economic, and political systems. This requires a great shift: moving past the limitations we have learned about what's possible and unleashing our political imagination to achieve a bold, new vision.

I've always envisioned the book as a handbook—something people will mark up, throw in their backpack for easy reference, and take to meetings with colleagues or other community organizers. In that spirit, I created this journal and workbook. It is a companion to the full book, which contains powerful stories and important background information. The most important part is the practices. I call these practices "prescriptions," or "Rx's," because my background as a doctor working in public health has taught me that most ailments can be cured with the right prescription. I presented Revolutionary Optimism to the world as a cure for the hopelessness, cynicism, and despair I've observed both in myself and all around me. By using the Rx's, Revolutionary Optimism becomes more than just another good idea. The practices, and the actions they inspire, are where the rubber meets the road. With that in mind, I've collected them all in this easy-to-use journal and workbook.

Additionally, I've added some discussion questions for those using this workbook with groups. My greatest dream is that others will use these practices together, refine or alter them to serve their community best, and use them to support their own evolution and that of the campaigns they are working on. I created this workbook as a gift to those who are committed to putting Revolutionary Optimism into practice. Share it with your friends and with other like-minded and like-hearted people who dream of a brighter future for our children.

If you haven't yet read *Revolutionary Optimism*, or if you need a refresher, here is a brief overview of the 7 steps to becoming a love-centered activist—a way to both inner healing and outer transformation:

Step 1: It's Go Time!

Many of us feel paralyzed by the enormity of our daily lives and the world's challenges, and we struggle to find our place in the world. This step offers the tools you need to put love into action right away and have an impact from Day 1.

Step 2: Self-Liberation

Here, we lay the groundwork for freeing ourselves from inner oppression so that our efforts to liberate ourselves and the world will be most effective and whole. We also discover our unique path of service.

Step 3: Accessing Unify Consciousness

No problem can be solved at the level of consciousness that created it. In this step, we open ourselves to higher consciousness so that we may be infused with the divine peace, insight, and passion we need to create real transformation.

Step 4: Peace-Crafting

Now that we've laid the inner foundation for transformation within ourselves, it's time to engage with others. This step offers practices for healing separation and conflict between people—whether individuals or nations—and emerging into collaborations for mutual benefit.

Step 5: Imagineering

In this step, we unlock our political imagination to what's really possible. Then we explore how to build revolutionary, love-centered movements to turn our individual and collection visions into reality.

Step 6: Sparking Peaceful Revolutions

Here we dive into the strategy and tactics of peaceful resistance and nonviolent direct action. We explore the essential, practical tools that turn our passion for action into the power to make revolutionary transformation a reality.

Step 7: Unifying

Unifying brings together everything we've learned so far, and offers a path forward bringing together diverse people, ideas, and movements to work for our personal and collective liberation. You will have clear action steps to move forward confidently, knowing your efforts and desire for transformation will not be wasted.

How to Use This Journal & Workbook

You may use this journal and workbook on your own or with a group. I recommend bringing together people from your book club, volunteer group, workplace, spiritual community, gardening group, student group, or wherever else you find like-hearted people who want to make a change in the world.

You may wish to gather for seven meetings to go over each step in detail. Or you could pick your favorite practices from each step and go over it all in a few meetings. Alternatively, you could go through one practice and discussion before the start of your regular meetings, or at the end. Finally, you could simply work through it all on your own, using the discussion prompts as journaling exercises. You can deepen your experience of Revolutionary Optimism individually or with a group by doing one step each day over a week, or one step each week over seven weeks, or one step each month for seven months, or any other way you choose.

For each step, I offer a series of practices. Each practice is accompanied by a brief introduction. You may wish to read the introduction out loud if practicing in a group, and then take time to do the practice. There are discussion questions after each practice to support you in integrating the experience and strengthening your connection with others. I've offered many discussion questions for each practice—feel free to choose those that most interest you and leave the rest for another time.

Feel free to use this journal and workbook creatively in any way you see fit. It's here to support your growth as a Revolutionary Optimist.

REVOLUTIONARY OPTIMISM
Journal & Workbook

STEP 1
It's Go Time!

7 Steps for Living as a Love-Centered Activist

- STEP 2 Self-Liberation
- STEP 3 Accessing Unify Consciousness
- STEP 4 Peace-Crafting
- STEP 5 Imagineering
- STEP 6 Sparking Peaceful Revolutions
- STEP 7 Unifying

Step 1:
It's Go Time!

THE HARDEST part is getting started. So many people today are trapped by anxiety and hopelessness. The problems of the world seem too big for any one person to have an impact. But if we have the courage simply to try, to take simple actions that we hope will have some small impact today, we are often surprised by just how much change one person can make. All it takes is touching one person's life in a small way to rekindle the flame of optimism. We realize how easy it is to make a difference. Are we saving the world? Perhaps not. On the other hand, as Pete Seger once said, "I think the world will be saved by millions of small things." Perhaps we can each become one of those "millions of small things."

So, how do you begin? I recommend you start by making your own dreams and your feelings of hope about the future some of your biggest priorities. They go hand in hand with the optimism that you're stepping into. Imagine what might be possible—what you will have the energy and inspiration to do—as you begin to feel uplifted and even renewed. Envisioning a better future and welcoming positive feelings are some of your greatest resources and will add to every part of your life. In this section, you will go through three simple exercises that will activate your bold vision and give you the first essential steps to take on your path of Revolutionary Optimism.

Rx #1: How Can I Serve Today?

Every day, we navigate a variety of needs and responsibilities that often seem to be in direct competition with one another. Many of us have jobs, children, aging parents, pets, and other responsibilities aside from our commitment to solve climate change, racial injustice, or other pressing issues. Being an effective change agent means tending to all of these roles and responsibilities in balance. Rather than viewing them as compartmentalized aspects of our lives, I think it's helpful to see them as four concentric circles of service that flow into each other and that we can engage with at any time:

We live at the center of these circles, and each of the four is vital to our path of service. Yet it's important to tend to the closest circle first—self. If you are nearing the edge of exhaustion, take the day off and do whatever recharges you on a deep level. If a family member is sick or in distress, be there for them. Channel all your love for the world and all your desire to make change into *that* act of service. Show up fully now, and you'll be able to show up fully in the wider circles too.

Showing up fully in each moment that presents itself will naturally expand your ideas about how to serve. That means responding to what is happening right here and now, not operating from a predetermined checklist. When most people think of activism, they typically think only of the last two circles: community and world. However, these are often addressed at the expense of the first two. Self-care and self-love, in tandem, are top priorities that can help you prevent health problems, burnout, and outright giving up. The second circle, your loved ones, is essential to prioritize in order to maintain strong and healthy relationships. This is the sweetness of life, after all. When our relationships suffer—and more specifically, when the people we cherish suffer—so does our ability to be of service in any capacity. None of us can drive transformation on our own. We just do better together.

These days, when I ask myself, "How can I serve?" I explore what care I need first. Then, if I'm in a place where I can go beyond self-care, I seek to provide family and friends with loving support. Then I move into serving my wider community and the world as a whole. Of course, these spheres are all interconnected. Self, loved ones, community, and world all affect each other. And we're certainly not limited to tending to only one of these circles a day. Again, when we're taking good care of ourselves, we are better able to give, to support, and to put our love into action.

Ask the Sacred Question: How Can I Serve Today?

1. Begin by focusing on your breath. Become aware of your breath as an ever-present companion. Then imagine this companion as a force larger than yourself—a universal breath that was here before you were born and will go on after you have stopped breathing. Imagine the breath as the energy of the Great Mystery and allow it to breathe through you. Then, relaxing even more, allow *it* to "breathe" *you*.
2. From this place of openness, ask the question, "How can I serve today?" Notice and welcome the intuitions and guidance you receive.
3. Explore the first of the four circles: self. Ask, "What would it look like to put love at the center of self-care today?" Honestly evaluate your needs and capacity. If you are running low on energy, if you're feeling stretched or overwhelmed, stop here and spend your time tending to your needs. If you feel well-resourced and self-care requires a smaller portion of your energy, move on to the second circle.
4. Ask, "What would it look like to put love at the center with my loved ones today? How can I serve them?" If there is great need in this circle, stop here. If there are fewer needs and you have the capacity to do more, move on to the next circle.
5. Ask, "What would it look like to put love at the center with my community today? How can I serve them?" If there is great need in this circle, stop here. If there are fewer needs and you have the capacity to do more, move on to the next circle.
6. Ask, "What would it look like to put love at the center of my relationship with my wider community, my country, or my global community? How can I serve my larger human family or my environment?"

Group Discussion Questions

1. Which of the ways of serving are easiest for you?
2. Which of the ways of serving do you find yourself avoiding or neglecting?
3. How has this practice inspired you to explore new ways of serving?
4. How can our group identify ways in which we can serve together?
5. What actions can the group take together?
6. Can the group create shared structures of collaboration?
7. Can your group explore this question again and again?

Rx #2: Making Commitments

Commitment is the antidote to confusion, caution, and complacency. I believe this is because commitment is our love made visible, our love *demonstrated*—which effectively dissolves those roadblocks. And what feels more uplifting than giving the best of ourselves? Not perfectly, but wholeheartedly. Perhaps it's the power of this love that gives us the courage to work through our fears and take actions that are aligned with our values. It lifts us up, giving us the tenacity and drive to keep going, no matter what challenges arise.

A timeless touchstone that reminds of the power of commitment is the teaching of German philosopher Johann Wolfgang von Goethe, who said:

> Until one is committed, there is hesitancy, the chance to draw back. Concerning all acts of initiative (and creation), there is one elementary truth that ignorance of which kills countless ideas and splendid plans: that the moment one definitely commits oneself, then Providence moves too. All sorts of things occur to help one that would never otherwise have occurred. A whole stream of events issues from the decision, raising in one's favor all manner of unforeseen incidents and meetings and material assistance, which no [person] could have dreamed would have come [their] way. Whatever you can do, or dream you can do, begin it. Boldness has genius, power, and magic in it. Begin it now.

My Commitments

1. Bringing a notebook or journal with you, find a quiet place where you won't be interrupted. Take a seat and begin with a breathing practice to center yourself.
2. Ask yourself, "Of all the issues in my life and in the world today, what speaks to me the most right now?" Follow your intuition and observe where the greatest amount of energy is stirring. There may be many things that speak to you but choose just one for now.
3. Be aware of any thoughts you may have about the issue being overwhelming or unfixable. Observe these thoughts, recognizing that it's natural for them to arise, but don't invest in them. Recognize that they are just thoughts, they are not the truth. Imagine the possibility that the challenge can be solved.
4. Make a declaration: "I am committed to doing whatever I can to address this issue." Use specific language that names the issue and expresses your personal commitment to take action.
5. Write your declaration in your journal. Your commitment is now something that you can powerfully integrate into your life in the days and months

ahead. Now brainstorm as many specific actions as you can about what you're going to address and how. Writing it down takes it out of the realm of abstract thought and gives it concrete reality. Also, write down the fears that these steps bring up for you, acknowledging the full emotional terrain you're stepping into.

6. Consider steps that you'll need to take to follow through on your big, overarching commitment. What will you need to do this year? This month? This week? Write these down in your journal and make a commitment to begin the first step today. You may need to split some action steps into smaller chunks to make them more doable. When necessary, make them small enough that you'll be sure to do them—even if it's something as simple as sending one email. Creating the momentum of action is what's most important.

7. Tell one other person about your commitment. Doing this helps bring your commitment from the personal realm to the interpersonal. It also begins or strengthens the vital practice of connecting with others—for none of us can transform the world on our own.

8. Take the first action.

9. Each day in your journal, write down what steps you took to honor your commitment and what you learned. Notice how your quest to change the world is also making changes in you.

GROUP DISCUSSION QUESTIONS

1. What issue did you choose to commit your energy and attention to, and why?
2. What is the first action you chose? How did it feel to make a commitment to take that action?
3. How do you hold yourself accountable for the actions that you commit to take?
4. As a group, how can we support one another in our personal commitments to take action?
5. Can our group commit to taking action together?
6. Think of an experience of when "providence" created opportunities when you made a commitment. Share this experience with the group.
7. Imagine that the moment you are in right now is a taste of providence!

Rx #3: Imagining Future Generations

A vision of a person or people from a future generation can galvanize your commitment to take actions on the causes that matter to you. It can recharge you and lift you into "action mode" to explore all the ways you can serve on behalf of future generations. Sometimes our vision needs to grow to give us a larger mission—one that stretches our capacity to contribute while also giving us a big enough "why" to sustain the energy it will take to see it through. I offer you a practice that has done this for me and can do the same for you.

> ### Imagining Future Generations
>
> 1. Begin by finding a comfortable seated position in a place free from distractions. Close your eyes and pay attention to your breath.
> 2. Think of someone in your own life who you love and cherish: a child, family member, or friend. If possible, choose someone much younger than yourself.
> 3. Imagine them in their old age, looking back at you. Imagine that in this future, humanity is living in a healthy and balanced way, the climate emergency has been tackled, and, through the generations, we have created a sustainable and peaceful global community together.
> 4. Open yourself up to receive whatever message they might have for you. Imagine that they are thanking you for the choices you made and the actions you took to create a beautiful and just world. Allow them to describe in detail the pivotal actions and choices that made the most significant difference.
> 5. Now imagine this one person surrounded with others of their generation, as well as their children and grandchildren. Imagine that beside you are many other people of your own generation, all working for the healing and liberation of all life. Imagine that as a group, the future generations are giving thanks to all those of your generation who stood up for life. Recognize that even though you may not know each other, you are part of a community working for the healing of the world.
> 6. Thank the members of future generations and say goodbye for now. Now choose one action aligned with that vision that you can take today. Do it now or plan a specific time when you will do it a little later today.

Group Discussion Questions

1. What was your experience of doing the Imagining Future Generations practice?
2. Which person did you imagine in the future?
3. What perspectives did you gain from imagining this person talking and guiding you from the future?
4. What legacy do you wish to leave for future generations?
5. What steps can you take over the next 30 days to create the future you wish to see?
6. What experiences did people in the group have when sharing this practice with others?
7. How can our group use the future generations practice to inspire each other and stay motivated to accomplish our commitments for action?

REVOLUTIONARY OPTIMISM
Journal & Workbook

STEP 2
Self-Liberation

STEP 1 — It's Go Time!
STEP 3 — Accessing Unify Consciousness
STEP 4 — Peace-Crafting
STEP 5 — Imagineering
STEP 6 — Sparking Peaceful Revolutions
STEP 7 — Unifying

7 Steps for Living as a Love-Centered Activist

Step 2: Self-Liberation

IF YOU have ever felt unvalued by others, unheard, misunderstood, powerless, or like you're not good enough to achieve what you want to, then we are part of a club, because I certainly have felt those things too. When I allow myself to become overwhelmed by negative experiences and feelings, I cease to practice the attitude that brings hope and salvation to my spirit, and I fall into despair. Fortunately, that happens less and less. I've found a path that has allowed me to transform difficulties into a fuel that drives me forward along a positive path.

There are two main forces that cause suffering and limit our ability to be genuinely hopeful. The first one is a lack of clarity about our life purpose and what we feel passionate about. Without this knowing, it's all too easy to allow other people to define our path for us. When we're not pursuing our purpose, whatever we're doing is not sustainable in the long term. The second is the host of psychological and emotional challenges we all face, which I refer to collectively as the "inner dragon." When I allow myself to be limited by what others believe I can or should do (or more often, what I *shouldn't* do), my capacity for service becomes limited. Likewise, when I'm overcome by my own inner turmoil, I become irritable, unmotivated, reactive, and ineffective.

Happily, I've discovered that there is a way out of this suffering and limitation. There are simple tools and practices that any of us can use to tame our inner dragon and find more and more freedom as we unlock our ability to have our greatest impact on our world.

In this section, I'll share two practices that have been essential companions for me on my path to self liberation.

Rx #4: Finding Your Soul's Deployment

One of the most powerful actions we can take towards self-liberation is to find the work that we are uniquely called to do. I call this "choosing how to be deployed," or finding our life purpose.

Since there are countless causes worthy of our time, many of us wonder how to make the right choice. If you feel this way, consider asking yourself the question, "Where do I feel the most passion?" Passion *always* leads us along the path to purpose. The activities that light us up are what inspire our greatest creativity and most courageous actions. They reveal to us our "inner blueprint," which contains our greatest potential for service. To paraphrase the author and theologian Frederick Buechner, you will find your purpose where your greatest passion meets the world's greatest need.

I have made the mistake of doing what I thought I "should do" rather than following my passion. The result was time wasted on projects that never came to fruition. I've gradually learned that when I follow what I'm sincerely passionate about, doorways open up where I never would have expected them to, and I have the energy and drive to create far greater change than if I were still following the dreary path of "shoulds." When I engage in what I'm uniquely suited to do, not only am I a more effective agent of transformation, but I also enjoy the process so much more. If this isn't your current experience, I want this for you, too—to feel the kind of deep fulfillment that can only come from doing what stokes your inner flame of aliveness to a roaring fire. In this exercise, you will explore your life purpose—what I call, "Finding your soul's deployment."

Finding Your Soul's Deployment

Defining your life purpose is an ongoing journey. At different points in your life, its definition will become more nuanced and your understanding will evolve. The question, "What is my life purpose?" isn't something you ask once. You ask it many times along your journey.

1. Create an intention to find your life's purpose. Acknowledge that you are part of a history of your family, including the lineage of your ancestors, and you carry gifts for the world that only you can give. Be open to receiving guidance about the right next step.
2. Ask, "What makes me excited so that I feel it in my body?" Follow your intuition and discern what excites you at your core. What gives you chills

up and down your spine? What gives you more energy? What does your gut tell you about your interests? If new subjects or career pathways are starting to interest you, follow them. Your parents, peers, spouse, and children do not get to decide for you. You are in the driver's seat of your life. Remember, if you are making choices based on the expectations of others, your choices may be misaligned with your true purpose.

3. Create opportunities for experimentation. We discover and learn by doing. Join clubs, seek out fellowships, travel far and wide, pursue your interests, and see if they continue to excite you. The key is to not wait around for the perfect situation or opportunity, but rather to take action and treat each step as an experiment. Keep asking, "Which parts of this feel like me and which parts don't?"

4. Repeat the above steps. We have the opportunity to constantly restructure our lives and shape-shift. It's healthy. Whenever you feel stuck, trapped, or forced, use those uncomfortable feelings as guideposts. They will show you the way out, where you have the joyous freedom to reinvent yourself again and again.

GROUP DISCUSSION QUESTIONS

1. What are the unique gifts that you carry?
2. Focus on each person in the group in turn. What do others in the group observe as the unique gifts they carry?
3. How have your life experiences inspired you to be of service?
4. What are the different ways that your soul is being deployed?
5. What are the different ways that people in the group understand how their souls are being deployed? Are there any patterns within the group?
6. What experiences did people in the group have when sharing this practice with others?
7. Can you share the practice of defining your soul's purpose in your daily life with others at your home, workplace, and in your communities?

Rx #5: In the Event of a Trigger: Respond with Love

One of the most life-changing opportunities in the quest to "know how we tick" is to intentionally seek to understand our emotional triggers. Triggers are situations and circumstances that provoke intense and sometimes overwhelming negative emotions. In an instant, they can catapult emotions way out of proportion to a given situation, so it's important to learn to manage them.

When we act from being triggered—hyper-emotionally and disproportionately—we can end up saying or doing things we regret. We may act out in ways that are harmful to ourselves and others. We've all seen children have temper tantrums. In a very real way, our triggers bring out our emotionally immature selves. That is why it's so important to understand what it feels like to be triggered—so that we can allow that triggered feeling or sensation to act as a signal. The signal says: *Stop, take a deep breath, and maybe take some physical space from the conversation or situation that you're feeling triggered by.*

Neuroscience tells us that the human brain responds to triggers in four possible ways: flight, fight, freeze, or appease. Fighting can take the form of yelling, speaking with the intention to harm, or even physical confrontation. Flight means simply leaving the situation altogether. When we freeze, we become non-responsive. Lastly, when we try to appease, we fawn over or placate dangerous people or situations to try to give the bully or abuser what they want.

Our moments of being triggered, as challenging as they are, are potentially some of our greatest growth experiences: opportunities to find the tender places within us that need more care. Therefore, it's important to remember not to judge ourselves when we become triggered. Each trigger that comes up shows us a part of ourselves that needs love. Anger, for instance, often arises out of a desire to keep ourselves safe, as a mask to protect the hurt part of us that is just below the surface. Because triggers are often born out of trauma, the answer isn't to tamp them down or feel bad about ourselves for having them, but instead to treat ourselves with great kindness and care. The gift of our triggers is found when we consciously seek out and find the aspects of ourselves that feel unsafe or unloved—*and love them*. This is how we put love at the center when a wounded part of us would rather lash out with words of anger or throw a chair through a window. This is how we "manage" our triggers.

Learning to manage our reactions is not easy, but love makes it possible. Then we are able to stop wasting time on the small stuff and have energy available for what matters most to us.

Lastly (and this is big), managing our triggers asks us to take 100 percent responsibility, without guilt or shame, for our part in what occurred. We can't change anyone else's behavior, and we can always heal and transform ourselves.

In the Event of a Trigger...

1. **Take a break:** When you're in a triggered state, that's not the time to have an important conversation, make a point in a meeting, or talk to a legislator (yes, I learned the hard way). Taking a break interrupts the chain of triggers that can derail any conversation and gives the cortisol (that chemical that causes us to fight or flee) surging through your system a chance to subside. You want to be the best version of yourself when you are communicating to catalyze bold transformation.

2. **Grow in awareness:** Become aware of outside forces that are causing you to be in a heightened state of negative emotions, ripe for a meltdown. That means you might need to turn off the news or limit your daily exposure, avoid the doomsayer friend who makes your blood pressure spike, and delegate conversations with a particularly difficult colleague to someone who isn't annoyed by them.

3. **Study yourself:** Learn to identify the patterns of when and how you are triggered—who you find triggering, what circumstances set you off, and what the negative effects of being triggered are. Be aware of your reactions, your patterns, and the underlying beliefs you may have that match up with them.

4. **Study others:** If you sense the person you are trying to build bridges with is being triggered—maybe by you—that is an opportunity for you to respond compassionately. Rather than getting triggered yourself and escalating a difficult situation, see if you can feel understanding towards the person who is starting to get upset. You will never regret making this effort.

5. **Don't assign blame:** It's easy to blame other people for our emotional reactions, but we do have a choice. So I recommend bringing your awareness back to yourself and remember the idea that at least 80 percent of your reactions are about what's going on inside of *you*. Blame is a painful mindset to hang out in, and it never leads to the generative outcomes that a Revolutionary Optimist aspires to.

For more information, check out the Managing Your Triggers Toolkit. You can download the articles in this series, and other tools, at: atctools.org/resources/tools-for-transformation

Group Discussion Questions

1. How do you respond when you are triggered? Which of the four reactions is your default?
2. Are you always aware when you are triggered? What are your blindspots?
3. Consider the last time you acted from a place of being triggered. How could you have acted differently if you'd had greater awareness of that trigger? What impact might that have had on the outcome of the situation?
4. Consider one of your greatest triggers. What unhealed part of yourself is calling to be integrated and loved? How can you begin to practice loving this part?
5. What type of triggers do people in the group have in common?
6. What experiences did people in the group have when sharing this practice with loved ones, friends, and coworkers?
7. How can the group support each member to be aware of when they are triggered and how they respond?

STEP 3
Accessing Unify Consciousness

STEP 2 Self-Liberation

STEP 4 Peace-Crafting

STEP 1 It's Go Time!

STEP 5 Imagineering

7 Steps for Living as a Love-Centered Activist

STEP 7 Unifying

STEP 6 Sparking Peaceful Revolutions

Step 3:
Accessing Unify Consciousness

IN ORDER to create a world of justice and peace, we must approach solving the current crises from a higher level of consciousness. That means that each of us is invited to engage in practices that expand our awareness as individuals and ignite the spark of our collective divinity, which we all carry within. Only then can we have access to the full wisdom, insight, and stamina needed to create a world in which unifying is possible. This is where unify consciousness enters the room.

Unify consciousness is an awareness of our interconnectedness with all life and with a loving force sourced from within our own hearts. The love force is an awareness that holds, soothes, and uplifts all living beings. While it is called by many names—collective consciousness, unity consciousness, Christ consciousness, Buddha mind, Krishna consciousness, messianic consciousness, satori, mystical experience, nature mysticism, hallelujah consciousness, and so on—the experiences and their effects are similar.

As a felt experience, unify consciousness sparks an awareness and sensations in my body affirming that I am interconnected with all of humanity, and all life, including our ancestors and descendants. I am experiencing that we are all divine sparks from one source—a love force that flows through the universe. Recognizing and appreciating the gorgeous diversity of beliefs and ideologies that humans have is an opportunity to see the manifestations of creation with curiosity. From this vantage point, our differences bind us together, rather than separate us.

In order to cocreate this epic phase of human experience into a truly transformational moment in history, we must start to identify with life as a whole—with all people and all beings everywhere. This means letting go of the game of "good and bad," of "us vs. them," and work together on behalf of all life. In this section, you'll find practices that help you do just that.

Rx #6: Breathe to Connect

Anyone who is engaged in radically transformative work needs a powerful practice to keep in their pocket, capable of opening their heart to greater awareness in times of need. And one of the most accessible and powerful practices I know of relies on one thing we will never be without for as long as we're alive: our breath.

Our breath is literally our lifeline. It's a traveling companion that is always with us. It's also the thread that connects our "small selves" to the "larger self" of unity and interconnection. By becoming aware of our breath, we relax. Then we can use simple visualizations to open ourselves further to the peace, wisdom, and unity of the Great Mystery.

Connecting with our breath is one of the fastest and most effective doorways to higher states of consciousness. Here is a simple practice that combines breathing with connecting with the heavens, earth, and waters—reminding us of our interconnectivity with all of existence.

Heaven, Earth, and Water Breathing

1. Sitting tall, position yourself with your feet on the ground, your back erect, and your hands in your lap.
2. Breathe in through your nose, into your heart space. Know that your breath is filling you with life and energy, expanding your inner stillness. As you do, be aware of your heart space expanding. Then breathe out through your mouth. Repeat this several times.
3. Take another deep breath into your heart. As you breathe out, this time imagine the energy traveling upward, through the top of your head and out the crown. Sense your exhalation floating up into the atmosphere, into the ever-expanding universe.
4. Then breathe in and fill your expanding heart space again with your breath that is now infused with the love energy from the entire universe. As you do this, allow yourself to receive all the peace and wisdom that holds the vast universe together.
5. Take another breath in. Now breathe out slowly, imagining this energy going down, down, down, through your body, into the earth below you. Your breath travels through the earth's crust, past the mantle, and all the way down to the molten core at the center of the earth. As you breathe in again, bring the wise and loving energy of the earth up into your heart space. When you do this, you are grounding yourself into the deep center of the earth and recharging yourself with the universal energy field.

6. Breathe into your heart space. Breathing out, send energy down into the aquifers under the land. Feel the interconnected waters that flow beneath the earth. Place all of your attention in this moment on *water*, which is the source of all life. On your next in-breath, imagine that concentrated life energy flowing upwards from the waters below the surface of the earth, filling your heart space with this luminous energy.
7. Repeat this practice as many times as you like, filling your heart space with this cycling breathing—moving fluidly between the heavens, the earth, and the waters.

GROUP DISCUSSION QUESTIONS

1. What was your experience with the breathing practices?
2. How do you use breathing practices to connect with the sacred as part of your daily life?
3. What is one place in your life that you could use this practice to transform the way you show up? What might change if you did so?
4. What body sensations or mental images did you experience after doing the breathing practice?
5. Can the group consider starting with a breathing practice at the beginning of each gathering?
6. What experiences did people in the group have when sharing this practice with others?
7. Can you bring a routine breathing practice into your daily life at your home, workplace, and in your communities?

Rx #7: Chanting Praise

I offer you one of my favorite daily practices—a chanting practice that awakens love energy through music and singing. This practice is a pathway for accessing higher consciousness.

Chanting Praise, which I also call the "Hallelujah Chant," is a way to offer praise for this present moment—for being alive, for being where we are, for having whatever experience we are having, without judgment. Chanting is a call and response between ourselves and the Divine. It reminds us that the Great Mystery, the Unknowing, the Universe—or whatever word you prefer to use to describe your higher power—is acknowledging our journey and the beauty of who we are and who we are becoming.

When I take the time to do some simple breathing exercises (as we explored together in the previous chapter) followed by chanting to center myself in the present moment, I supercharge myself as a loving presence in the here and now. This combination is so powerful! It wakes up every cell of my being, where it becomes effortless to channel the overflow of my love to all people and all life. I feel in touch with the universe and its unending possibilities.

As you can tell, this practice is fuel for the greatest of Revolutionary Optimism—the kind that can fuel peaceful and profound revolutions, internally and externally. When I approach life with my own version of this optimism, I am able to see past my flaws, imperfections, and shortcomings, understanding that I and each person I encounter throughout the day is a pure soul and worthy of being seen with new eyes and an open heart.

The Eyes of Infinite Possibility

I close my eyes to chant. When I open them afterwards, I am living in the present moment and seeing the beauty in the world. Breathing and chanting, even if I just do it for a few quick minutes at the beginning of a day that may be packed with stress, teaches me to invite inner joy while simultaneously maintaining full awareness of the suffering in the world. I can hold both—"this" *and* "that."

I love the word *and*. It's a word that keeps open the realm of possibility—especially that which lies beyond what I've yet imagined. At the beginning of each day, I am aware of all of the suffering and the pain in the world, *and* I also see the beauty and overall goodness—a joy field. It's possible for the full awareness of beauty to ease the pain.

Acknowledging joy and feeling gratitude doesn't close us off to the pain in the world. In truth, it can help us feel or sense the grief, anguish, and despair of others even more because our hearts are open. I know now that two things (many things, in fact) can be true at the same time. I can see both the pain and the hopefulness of our human family and let all of that matter to me. Then I care enough to do something about it. I want to ease the pain and unleash the hope.

With that in mind, let's chant.

Hallelujah Practice

Opening suggestions: As for a sacred word, if you it feels good to you, you can simply sing the word *Hallelujah*, or repeat it silently within. As you chant "Hallelujah"—the Hebrew word for *praise*—you are giving praise and receiving praise from the Great Mystery. Also, feel free to play with the melody and cadences. For example, you could use Leonard Cohen's version, Handel's, or create your own.

1. Prepare yourself by setting an intention.
2. Begin singing "Hallelujah." Imagine your heart opening more and more with each repetition. Give praise to the Great Mystery and all life.
3. Now allow yourself to *receive* praise from the Great Mystery itself—feeling honored for all that you are and all that you're becoming; being praised for your whole journey, all the good, the bad, and the ugly. Practice receiving praise and allowing it to move through you, allowing your wholeness to be shared with the world.
4. After repeating the chant for five minutes (or as long as you wish), become silent. Sit in the stillness.

GROUP DISCUSSION QUESTIONS

1. What did it feel like to offer praise? What did it feel like to *receive* praise from the Great Mystery?
2. What body sensations or mental images did you experience after doing a praise practice?
3. What role might this kind of ecstatic praise play in advocacy work and activism?
4. What would it look like to integrate praise into your daily life?
5. Can you imagine a difficult situation where you may respond with a silent, internal praise practice so that you can help center yourself? What might transpire if you respond this way?
6. What experiences did people in the group have when sharing this practice with others?
7. Can the group explore bringing chants, freedom songs, music, and art into all aspects of their lives?

Rx #8: Silly Sneeze Practice

According to Sri Swami Satchidananda, "Laughter is the best medicine no matter the illness." I always say that laughter is the common human language—no matter where you are, people love to laugh. No matter how difficult things are, people still find things to laugh about. Our resiliency in this way is astonishing. We can go through incredibly difficult passages while still seeing the beauty and absurdity of life.

Studies have shown that laughing has a host of physical and psychological benefits. Laughing oxygenates the blood, releases endorphins, produces more T cells to boost our immunity, and increases self-confidence. Each one of these outcomes is reason enough to actively *pursue* laughter. Why wait? This is where a tool like Laughing Yoga can be a game-changer—and I have a little story to show you how.

Laughing Yoga is a practice that you can do by yourself or in groups. To practice it, all you have to do is start laughing until you get to the point where you're laughing hysterically at yourself. Most people have to pretend at first. It's OK to "fake it 'til you make it." Studies have shown that even if you're not authentically or spontaneously laughing, endorphins are being released. Those positive hormones make you feel good when you're laughing, and they continue to float around in your body and brain when you stop laughing.

I suggest starting off with a five-minute practice each day. You can practice while you're in the shower, driving to work, or whenever you're by yourself.

Laughing Yoga allows groups of all kinds to step out of collective despair and create a new energy. And of course the type of groups that benefit from Laughing Yoga includes families and friends.

Silly Sneeze Practice

This practice is to be done with a partner or with a group of people.

1. Make eye contact with your partner.
2. Both you and your partner pretend that you're sneezing. As part of finishing up each sneeze, you force yourself to break out into laughter. To start with, just pretend to laugh with each sneeze—"fake it 'til you make it."
3. Let yourself enjoy the giggles and the surges of energy that accompany this silliness. Let yourself get sillier and louder! Notice what absurd

creatures humans can be. Embrace the beauty in our fallibility; our imperfections; our goofiness.
4. As the energy of the group peaks, invite everyone to simultaneously invoke childhood playfulness by everyone clapping their hands and shouting, "Very good, very good!" Then throw your arms and hands up in the air and shout, "Yay!"

Special Note: Laugh-a-Yoga and Laughter Yoga International are great resources for learning more and getting yourself certified in this fun practice.

GROUP DISCUSSION QUESTIONS

1. Do you ever become over-serious? What is the impact of that on your life and your ability to make change?
2. What was your experience of the silly sneeze practice? How did the practice make you feel?
3. What body sensations or mental images did you experience after doing the silly sneeze practice?
4. What is the role of joy and laughter in your life as a love-centered activist?
5. Can you imagine ways that you can bring laughter into your everyday life? Or into a close relationship, or into your family?
6. Can the group cocreate their own laughing yoga practice for routine use?
7. Can the group explore innovative ways of bringing laughing yoga into movement-building experiences?

STEP 4
Peace-Crafting

STEP 3
Accessing Unify Consciousness

STEP 5
Imagineering

7 Steps for Living as a Love-Centered Activist

STEP 2
Self-Liberation

STEP 6
Sparking Peaceful Revolutions

STEP 1
It's Go Time!

STEP 7
Unifying

Step 4:
Peace-Crafting

*[T]he holiest place on earth is where an
ancient hatred has become a present love.*
—A Course in Miracles

AS YOU walk the path of the Revolutionary Optimist with me, you will learn that moving the needle towards peace is about handling everything—from minor disagreements between allies to generational conflicts between peoples and countries—by putting love at the center. This means being curious about opposing viewpoints, investigating our own assumptions and beliefs, being discerning about all the information we take in, and being open-hearted in the face of interpersonal challenges. In order to build a new world, we must face conflict and disagreement head on and transform it into peace. I call this process peace-crafting.

Peace-crafting is the guiding star on the compass of Revolutionary Optimism. It is the art of working with others to bring forward transformative solutions. To do this, we use a methodology I will lay out for you that calls for honoring different perspectives and countering the polarization that is happening around and within us. Peace-crafting is the antidote to the small battles all around us—the endless conflicts on social media, the surface-level political slogans, and the dinner-table arguments with relatives. It is also a solution to the world's greatest wars and conflicts. It provides a path through these disagreements that leads to individual growth and unity between people. Making peace sometimes includes strong and even fierce love. This is the benevolent fire that can melt rigidity, aggression, and other forms of control.

We can use openness and dialogue as a more effective way to share our perspectives. When we approach others with a generosity of spirit that allows for truth-telling and mutual sharing, it's like knocking on the door of our neighbor's home versus forcing the door open. Waiting for the neighbor to open the door and invite us in might lead to a rich conversation over tea. Forcing the door open might lead to getting arrested, or worse.

Peace-crafting means establishing ourselves in a peacemaking role whenever life presents us with the opportunity. It involves understanding all points of view and working with both sides to establish ourselves as a credible intermediary, building trust with all parties, and working together towards transformative solutions, even as we identify with one particular point of view or perspective. The key is to focus on the good of the whole rather than only our own agenda, and to demonstrate equity, fairness, and true kindness as we strive for revolutionary transformation.

It is important to emphasize that the process of peace-crafting is cyclical, and not a linear sequence of events—it moves round and round in an endless circle of time as we strive to bend the arc of history towards justice. I have numbered the action steps for you as you read on in order to make them easy to track. However, rather than think of this as a linear prescription, I invite you to see it as a spiral adventure where each step takes you deeper into the truth of where peace is to be found.

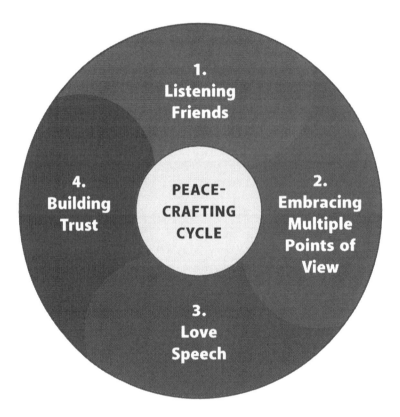

In this section, we explore a practice for deepening each aspect of the peace-crafting cycle, helping you to strengthen your ability to serve as the foundation of making peace with others.

Step 4: Peace-Crafting | 53

Rx #9: WAIT: Why Am I Talking?

The first peace-crafting action is to practice being a listening friend. Before going into a conversation, we can set the intention by asking ourselves: am I going into this as a listening friend? We can use this question to check ourselves in the midst of a conversation and shift quickly from being distracted to focused. We can also use it to reflect on why a conversation might not have gone as well as expected.

The most important time to use this practice is when we're interacting with those who have opposing viewpoints. Rather than activating somebody's defenses, we can disarm them through listening. Then, with both hearts open, we can proceed to have a meaningful dialogue.

We can allow ourselves to be changed by the other, just as they might allow themselves to be changed by us. This can only happen when we have deeply listened, heard, and had the strength of heart to let another guide us to higher ground. It's one of the greatest acts of love that I know.

In the world of the revolutionary optimist, being a listening friend is about allowing ourselves to open to the wisdom, guidance, and sometimes uncomfortable insights that unify consciousness offers. The more we say yes to being guided by this immense force of love, the greater positive impact we will have.

WAIT—Why Am I Talking?

While working in Africa, I learned my favorite Zambian expression: "Jaw-Jaw." It's similar to the American saying, "All talk, no action," and it refers to the human habit of speaking for the sake of speaking, talking over or interrupting people, and basically dominating others by talking—all of which wastes time and energy, and divides people.

To address my own habit of speaking too much or talking over people, I learned a practice from a friend called "**W**hy **A**m **I T**alking?" or **WAIT**. It's a question I ask myself when I am in meetings with two or more people. I say "**WAIT**" to myself to give myself a few quick seconds to decide if I have something worth saying. This short pause allows me to reflect, listen to what is being said more carefully, and makes space for others to speak first. This is one way to ensure that each person has an equitable amount of time to share their views.

Here are the steps:

1. Before you speak, ask yourself, **Why am I talking?** Notice whether your answer feels true or feels like a justification.

2. Notice how much you're talking in a conversation. Ask yourself, **What percentage of the conversation is taken up by what I have to say? Are other people being silenced?**
3. Does my silent and loving presence communicate enough in this moment?
4. Am I smiling and providing nodding affirmations while listening?
5. Out of all the people present, consider whether *your* voice is the one most-needed now.
6. Choose deliberately whether to speak/keep speaking or when to step back and keep listening.

GROUP DISCUSSION QUESTIONS

1. Take a moment to reflect on your use of speech. Do you talk over people or neglect to give space to others? Do you avoid speaking up even when you know you should?
2. How do elements of power and privilege influence the way you speak or remain silent with others?
3. What power does deep listening have? How have you experienced this power in your own life?
4. During the next meeting of your group, ask each person to use the WAIT practice. Toward the end of the session, ask each person how it felt to assess whether or not they should talk, and how that changed the conversation of the group. Were you able to listen better?
5. Did the WAIT practice give more space for someone who is normally quiet or shy to actually speak up?
6. What experiences did people in the group have when sharing this practice with others?
7. Can the WAIT practice be used at home and in all the places where people are together?

Step 4: Peace-Crafting

Rx #10: Having Courageous Conversations

The second peace-crafting action we can take is to embrace multiple points of view. As we engage in transformational movements, it's more important than ever to recognize and honor the validity of multiple viewpoints. Time and time again, I have learned that no matter how right I believe I am, other people have points of view that are equally valid. If I dare to let down my defenses and truly listen, the result is greater connection. And real connection always opens the way to genuinely transformative solutions.

It is critically important to acknowledge upfront our privilege, positionality, and varying intersectional life experience and perspectives. By sharing these truths, we are better able to cocreate new love- and justice-centered ways of listening that may heal the wounds from all that humanity has endured through the past generations.

Despite the polarization of these times, there is an upswell of people, like you and me, who are tired of polarization: those who stay present and open through challenging conversations, who embrace nuance, and who can hold multiple perspectives simultaneously without abandoning their own views. It's the presence of love and wisdom rising in people to increase the possibility of a more cohesive, unified society—one whose great commitment is to the dignity and preservation of life.

Having Courageous Conversations

One of the best tools I've found for deepening my relationships and making peace with others is called Courageous Conversations, from the Art of Transformational Consulting website. I highly recommend you visit their website (https://atctools.org/toolkit_tool/courageous-conversations-toolkit) to take advantage of their full toolkit. For now, I'll simply summarize the five tips they offer for pursuing courageous conversations:

1. **Practice Deep Listening.** This not only helps the other person feel heard and valued, but it also gives us valuable information about who they are, what they need, and what we can do to generate solutions.
2. **Be Authentic.** This is about being fully honest with ourselves, and then transparent with others. While many of us have a habit of avoiding uncomfortable truths, a practice of authenticity builds trust and moves both parties towards genuine resolution.
3. **Practice Skillful Communication.** This is about staying open to multiple points of view, being present, and staying focused on creating generative outcomes.

4. **Deal with Breakdowns.** This is about dealing with breakdowns in the communication process. Breakdowns happen because of substantive issues or people issues. Substantive issues are those that have to do with the actual facts of the situation and can be dealt with creatively through collaboration. Our issues have to do with our behaviors, unwillingness to collaborate, and emotional reactions. These can be dealt with through positive relationship-building and deep listening.
5. **Ensure Good Completion.** This is about making sure things are clear and feel complete to everyone involved. You double-check that everyone is satisfied and has the same understanding of the agreements and next steps.

The full toolkit offers a much more comprehensive plan—go check it out!

Group Discussion Questions

1. Think of an example from your life of a difficult conversation that led to a positive outcome. What worked well about it? What lessons would you bring to future conversations?
2. Consider times when you have not been fully authentic during important conversations. What stopped you from sharing your truth? What was the impact?
3. Are there any courageous conversations you've known you need to have, but have been avoiding? What might be the result if you had them?
4. Break the group up into pairs, and actually practice a courageous conversation, where one person pretends they are the person you want to have this conversation with. Make sure you have time to switch, so both people can practice.
5. Did the practice session prepare you when you actually had a courageous conversation? Share your experiences and the impact of your courageous conversations.
6. What experiences did people in the group have when sharing this practice with others?
7. Can this practice be used at home and in all the places where you are together with others?

Rx #11: Practicing Love Speech

The third part of the peace-crafting cycle is about bringing full awareness to the manner in which we speak. Love speech is a way of communicating through words—whether spoken or written in a text or email—that acknowledges each person's highest self and their greatest potential. We slow down and speak or write deliberately, ensuring that each word we utter is healing and supportive of the other person and all of humanity. Each word carries a vibration of peace and love, keeping love at the center of all our words. Each word we utter matters. The intention behind our words matters. To me, this means committing myself to a lifelong practice of always speaking with a loving intent.

It's hard to practice Revolutionary Optimism if we see another as an enemy. Even if we are actively working in opposite directions, we can still see the person's highest self and potential when we're willing to look. If we speak to their highest self from our highest self and not our ego, we bypass our own judgment of them and can engage with them more fruitfully.

Paying attention to our inner state is equally as important. I've learned that if I'm activated or triggered and speaking from my inner dragon (or the ego), I'm at high risk of saying things that are harmful or shaming to the other person. On the other hand, when I'm feeling centered in love, I speak in ways that are healing and lead towards transformative solutions.

Practicing Love Speech

Love speech has the power to lift those who receive our words and to possibly transform their lives. These are important questions to ask so that we practice keeping love at the center of all. The bottom line is to listen from love and speak from love. Being aware of the perspective we're speaking from is essential. Before speaking, reflect on the following questions that you can ask yourself:

1. Am I about to say something because it will truly contribute to a better outcome, or because I want to be right?
2. Am I speaking with the intent of tearing somebody down, or with the hope of building greater unity?
3. Am I speaking a hard but necessary truth, or being overly critical?

It's important to be able to see both the more intimate, local perspectives and narratives, as well as the wider, global perspectives and narratives.

1. What is my privilege and positionality in relation to the people I'm speaking with?
2. What narratives do I hold compared to the narratives the people I'm speaking with may hold?
3. Am I speaking from my own perspective?
4. Am I widening my viewpoint to include the community?
5. Am I including those who have been marginalized or oppressed?
6. Am I opening my perspective wide enough to contain the whole world?

Group Discussion Questions

1. What was your experience of preparing to be fully aware so that you can practice love speech?
2. What are the hardest times for you to practice love speech?
3. How does your position or privilege affect your ability or motivations to use love speech in your conversation with your peers, your family, or your coworkers?
4. How can you use love speech in a conversation with someone with whom you completely disagree?
5. How can you use love speech when you are angry or triggered?
6. What did people in the group experience when they shared this practice with others?
7. Can the love speech practice be used in your home, workplace, and community?

Rx #12: Trust-O-Meter

Building trust is the fourth essential part of peace-crafting. In this age of polarization, many people think of trust as binary, like an on/off switch: either they do or do not trust you. Mistrust can be permanent, and people become blocked out or canceled. This was my approach for quite some time. I would trust a person or an organization until they did something I disagreed with, then *wham!* I'd slam the gavel of mistrust down, and that was the end of the relationship.

Over time, I've learned that this approach is less than useful. It leaves no room for human imperfections or nuance, and it limits the relationships I can have to those who I align with 100 percent. That's a small world to live in, and it limits my possibilities for creating change.

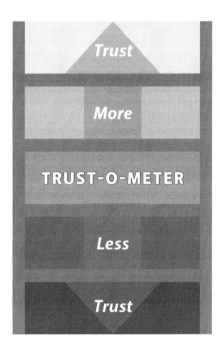

I have since found an approach that works better for me and my colleagues and produces better results in the work we do. We created the idea of the Trust-O-Meter. The Trust-O-Meter is dynamic: people can move up or down the ladder of trust, from deeply trusting to no trust. The foundation of the Trust-O-Meter is that everyone is a pure soul, worthy of love, even those we don't trust. It's an aid to help shift our perception and open our hearts—to see that a person's trustworthiness is not static, but rather, it can move up or down at any time. And no matter where someone is on the Trust-O-Meter ladder, there is an openness to engaging with them in some way appropriate to their level at a given time. There is always the possibility that they will move elsewhere on the ladder. Only in the most extreme cases is somebody blocked out completely (though this is sometimes necessary).

Trust-O-Meter

1. Begin by finding a comfortable seated position in a place free from distractions. Close your eyes and pay attention to your breath.
2. Think of or imagine someone in your own life whom you don't currently trust and you would like to explore how to rebuild your relationship.
3. Reflect on why there was a breakdown in trust and what role each person played in the breakdown.
4. What would need to happen to build trust with this person? What do they need to do? What do you need to do?
5. What kind of courageous conversation can you imagine that you need to have to rebuild trust with this person?
6. What are the reasons why you could never rebuild trust with this person?

GROUP DISCUSSION QUESTIONS

1. Do you have people in your life you don't trust? Can you imagine using the Trust-O-Meter to explore ways to rebuild trust?
2. What are the best ways to establish trust when you meet new people?
3. What are the best ways to reestablish trust when there has been a breakdown of trust? Is it better to avoid that person or to have a courageous conversation?
4. In the workplace, how can you apply the Trust-O-Meter with coworkers, supervisors, and/or organizational partners?
5. Share your positive and negative experiences of using the Trust-O-Meter in your life.
6. Can your group explore the Trust-O-Meter with your communities or movement-of-movements?
7. Can you group explore the Trust-O-Meter with groups that you don't agree with and have avoided any dialogue?

STEP 5
Imagineering

STEP 4 Peace-Crafting

STEP 6 Sparking Peaceful Revolutions

STEP 3 Accessing Unify Consciousness

7 Steps for Living as a Love-Centered Activist

STEP 7 Unifying

STEP 2 Self-Liberation

STEP 1 It's Go Time!

Step 5: Imagineering

STEP 5 is about imagining what is possible, then engineering a path to make it happen. I use the term *imagineering* to describe this process. First coined by Walt Disney in 1952, imagineering is defined here as "the process of bringing imaginative vision into reality." It is the integration of dreaming boldly with diligent work to transform those dreams into reality. As we pursue our individual aspirations, together we can harness the power of imagineering to shape a brighter future for all.

Clarity is the foundation of imagineering. We need to have a clear vision about where we're going in order to choose a good path forward—to avoid going down a rabbit hole that may not take us where we want to go. It's all too easy to jump into action with urgency without taking the time to reflect on what we're working towards. Like traveling with a map and compass in the great wilderness, clear vision enables us to move in the right direction—both as individuals and with movements involving many people.

Rx #13: Radical Imagination

As Revolutionary Optimists, we must have big dreams. If we seek only to improve the status quo, that's all we're going to do. But if we have a bold vision for greater transformation, our possibilities are limitless. We can think of the potential for change as the ocean, and the vision we hold as a vessel for carrying water. We can only experience as much transformation as our vessel—our vision—allows. Do you prefer to carry a vision the size of a teaspoon, or expand your vision to be as large as the ocean itself? I ask you this because I believe that you are here for a great reason, at a monumental time on our planet. And helping to unlock your imagination—politically and creatively—is the purpose in these pages.

Radical Imagination: Shaping What's Possible

In April 2023, Spring Strategies wrote, "Radical imagination is a tool social justice leaders and movements already use to collectively shape what's possible and to write new stories. As the Center for Story-based Strategy writes, 'We can only walk where our hearts have first tread.' But for many of us, the ability to access our imagination has been largely underutilized and untapped.

"According to Max Haiven, the author of *The Radical Imagination: Social Movement Research in the Age of Austerity*, radical imagination requires us to unlearn the dominant narratives that we've been taught—that there are no other alternatives to our current systems, structures, and the laws and policies that dictate who controls resources and how.

"Using our minds to move beyond these limiting frames and creating other possibilities is a decolonial process. In their book, *On Decoloniality*, professors Walter Mignolo and Catherine Walsh write, 'Decoloniality seeks to make visible, open up, and advance radically distinct perspectives and positionalities that displace Western rationality as the only framework and possibility of existence, analysis, and thought.'

"To suspend reality and create unique worlds in her artwork related to decolonizing aid, philanthropy, and knowledge, feminist artist Vidushi Yadav recommends starting by looking inward. She says, 'We have so much inside of us. We have our lived realities, our intergenerational knowledge that has been passed onto us orally by mothers, grandmothers, [our ancestors] about the lives they lived and challenges they faced to tap into.' If we can find the time and resources to journey into what she calls 'our heart space,' we have the possibility to find safety and peace—and use these individual experiences as a foundation to build upon and shape what's possible collectively."

Group Discussion Questions

1. What stops you from accessing your radical imagination?
2. Do you have any limiting beliefs or narratives that say that your boldest most radical imaginations are unrealistic or not possible?
3. Do you have people or communities in your life who encourage your radical imagination?
4. How can we decolonize our thinking so that we can unlock our imagination?
5. What are the ways in which oppressive social, economic, and political systems can obstruct our radical imagination?
6. Can your group consider having an imagineering meeting in your community?
7. What experience did people in the group have when sharing this practice with others?

Rx #14: What Are My Visions?

Evolutionary change is slow and gradual, like the movement of glaciers. Revolutionary change is sudden and nonlinear, like a wildfire. Understanding the difference between these two types of transformation is essential to developing a larger vision.

Neither evolutionary nor revolutionary transformation is better than the other. Both are necessary. However, there are times when the conditions are ripe for revolutionary transformation. When current systems fail to meet the needs of the people or to respond to the challenges we are facing, this requires revolutionary action. I believe that we are now living in revolutionary times.

During these revolutionary times, we cannot afford to accept that slow, incremental change is the only way forward. We must rise and boldly mobilize with others in our pursuit of a new world.

What Are My Visions?

Take your journal to a quiet place where you won't be disturbed. Do a centering breathing practice in preparation (see the "Heaven, Earth, and Water Breathing" Rx on p. 36, in Step 3). Then write on the following prompts:

- In my wildest dreams, what transformation would I like to see happen in the world?
- What is my legacy? How do I want to leave the world for future generations?
- How have I been limiting this vision? Have I been operating according to what I, others, or society consider realistic?
- What would it look like if I released all limitations?
- What would this transformation look like, specifically? (Paint a picture as vividly as you can.)
- What would it take to get there? What is the first step? How can I get started now? (List out all the necessary steps.)

GROUP DISCUSSION QUESTIONS

1. Share your experience of the journaling exercise with the group.
2. As each person in the group shares their vision, notice how you react to the boldest and bravest visions. What comes up for you?
3. How can you create spaces in your lives where unleashing your boldest visions can be nourished and encouraged?
4. How do you see the distinction between evolutionary visions and revolutionary visions?
5. Do you have a tendency to prefer evolutionary or revolutionary transformation?
6. Does your group have a mix of people who prefer evolutionary versus revolutionary transformation, or are you more aligned towards one approach?
7. How can your group practice courageous conversations with people who oppose or reject your visions?

Rx #15: Engaging Fear

Confronting our fears is an essential step in working for revolutionary transformation. As I take a stand for my beliefs, I know that I will be challenged by people with different perspectives. This is scary, especially when I feel alone. I also know that I will not be deterred. I am proud to say that I'm working every day to overcome all my fears and fully express myself as a Revolutionary Optimist.

By overcoming our fear and embracing our collective responsibility to care for the world, we can usher in an era of healing and repair. In this exercise, I invite you to explore your fears.

Exploring My Fears

Once again, take your journal to a quiet place where you won't be disturbed. Do a centering breathing practice in preparation (see the "Heaven, Earth, and Water Breathing" Rx on p. 36, in Step 3). Then write on the following prompts:

- What are my greatest fears?
- How do I believe that my fears will keep me safe?
- In what ways am I afraid of my own freedom?
- Do I seek external sources of authority to feel safe?
- How do I conform to family, community, and societal norms in order to be accepted by my community?
- What helps me overcome fear?
- Do I have a vision I am willing to die for? If I did, what might it be?

Group Discussion Questions

1. Share your experience of the journaling exercise with the group.
2. As each person shares their greatest fears, are there common fears that affect everyone?
3. What fears come from your own mind, your family, your community, your culture?
4. Are there things happening in your country or our world that are increasing fear for some people or for all people in your group?
5. Do you have people in your life with whom you feel comfortable sharing your fears?
6. Are you willing to make sacrifices to create the world that you want to see? What sacrifices are you willing to make?
7. Are you willing to die for your visions or beliefs? What comes up for you when you consider this question?

Step 5: Imagineering

Rx #16: Finding Your Role

As we develop our vision and explore ways to work together with others, it is critically important to prioritize where we devote our energy. It's important to choose wisely. If we try to be everything all the time, we'll end up accomplishing very little. While there are countless worthy causes that deserve our time, energy, and attention, the truth is that each of us has a full life, multiple responsibilities, and limited resources, and so we must focus our efforts. Prioritizing and determining the specific role we want to play in a given movement is the key. In this exercise, I offer a way to choose your next step—either as an individual, or as a movement.

Love-Centered Prioritization Criteria

I developed these Love-Centered Prioritization Criteria to determine what activities to work on as a movement leader. Since using it on a large scale, I've discovered that it works well for me personally, too—giving me clarity about how to organize my time by determining what is likely to have the most impact.

When considering which of the movements or campaigns I care about to invest my energy in, I take the time to consider how they rate on each of the criteria below. You can do this too. Just rate each campaign or action you're considering by each metric, with 1 being the lowest score and 5 being the highest. Tally up the total scores and compare them to see where your energy is best spent.

The following metrics can be used to evaluate any action you want to take or for any campaign you wish to begin. Read the following questions and rate them for yourself for each option that you are considering. Additionally, you can use these prioritization criteria with all kinds of planning groups.

Mission Metric: How closely does this action or campaign align with our vision, theory of change, priorities, and the projects that are already underway?

1   2   3   4   5

Impact Metric: Assessment of potential impact. How easy would it be to measure the potential impact? How much of an impact will this action or campaign have on desired goals?

1   2   3   4   5

Capabilities Metric: What capabilities are needed? What capabilities do I have, or do we have, to meet the needs? If certain capabilities are lacking, how can we get them? How capable are we to take this on? How much will this action or campaign increase, drain, or overwhelm our capabilities?

1   2   3   4   5

Low-Hanging-Fruit Metric: Low-hanging fruit are the quick wins that can be achieved because they have a lot of energy behind them already. Having success is essential for getting myself and others energized, though of course, it is never guaranteed. How confident are we that this will have a successful outcome?

1   2   3   4   5

Revolutionary Transformation Metric: Assessment of priorities that are essential to achieving the goals that others deem unrealistic or unachievable. These are the big goals that seem impossible to many—the foundation of revolutionary change. Is this an "impossible" change that just might work? Would this fundamentally change the game if successful? Am I (or are we) willing to struggle against the status quo?

1   2   3   4   5

Time-Sensitive Metric: Taking into account time-sensitive "windows of opportunity" that are upcoming, urgent, and timebound. Taking advantage of emergent opportunities. How important is it that this action happens now (or on the proposed timeline)?

1   2   3   4   5

Readiness Metric: Does this action or campaign increase readiness for whatever future scenarios may emerge as a result of the super-crises that are worsening? Does it build the capacity to deploy as needed based on circumstances? How ready are we to deal with the potential consequences of this action?

1   2   3   4   5

Tally up the points for any movements, campaigns, actions, or projects you're considering taking on. The one with the highest score is likely to be the best place for you to serve.

Group Discussion Questions

1. What were your results of the prioritization criteria?
2. Which of the criteria were the most important to you? How did that compare to others?
3. What did you learn about your own priorities by completing this exercise? Did you gain more clarity about your role or were you left more confused?
4. How has this exercise changed the way you and other group members determine priorities and choose roles?
5. Based on the prioritization criteria exercise, what are your next steps for taking action and why?
6. Can the prioritization criteria be used or adapted by an organization that you are working in? How could they help with decision-making?
7. What experience did people in the group have when sharing this practice with others?

REVOLUTIONARY OPTIMISM
Journal & Workbook

STEP 6
Sparking Peaceful Revolutions

STEP 5 Imagineering

STEP 7 Unifying

7 Steps for Living as a Love-Centered Activist

STEP 4 Peace-Crafting

STEP 1 It's Go Time!

STEP 3 Accessing Unify Consciousness

STEP 2 Self-Liberation

Step 6:
Sparking Peaceful Revolutions

OUR WORLD now is also in need of a heart transplant. We need a revolutionary miracle, and fast. We need to attempt a daring surgery in countries around the world to replace the dying systems of greed, hatred, oppression, and exploitation with those that are centered in love. We must create authentic democracies and life-sustaining systems fueled by compassion and justice.

Such miracles of social and political transformation are not easy or predictable, but they do happen. But something of a profound nature will only come to be if we are there to open the door to it—if we are awake, available, and ready. This often entails *doing something* that opens the door—taking action. We, the Revolutionary Optimists, can become the miracle that the world needs.

We can create historic social and political movements that bring all our ideas and efforts together so that we can unleash our creativity to transform. To do this, we need to be ready to rapidly respond when the conditions ripen for a revolutionary phase of transformation. We may have just enough time to do it if we act now.

This section gives you an introduction to some of the tools needed to spark a peaceful revolution.

Rx #17: Serve as Prophetic Witness

Dr. Martin Luther King Jr. defined nonviolence as "a love-centered way of thinking, speaking, acting, and engaging that leads to personal, cultural, and societal transformation." He described six principles of nonviolence to guide our personal exploration, which I'm adapting to include the use of "peaceful resistance" movements:

> **#1: Peaceful Resistance Is a Way of Life for Courageous People.** That is, peace and nonviolence are not the same as passivity—they are aggressive in that they actively resist evil and injustice. They are aggressive on a spiritual, mental, and emotional level.
>
> **#2: Peaceful Resistance Seeks to Win Friendship and Understanding.** Dr. King believed that the outcome of nonviolence is reconciliation and the creation of beloved community.
>
> **#3: Peaceful Resistance Seeks to Defeat Injustice, or Evil, Not People.** Dr. King recognized that evildoers are also victims and are not fundamentally evil people. He focused on defeating evil acts and systems and redeeming (rather than defeating) people.
>
> **#4: Peaceful Resistance Holds That Unearned, Voluntary Suffering for a Just Cause Can Educate and Transform People and Societies.** Peaceful resistance includes a willingness to voluntarily "turn the other cheek"—to accept suffering and harm without retaliating.
>
> **#5: Peaceful Resistance Chooses Love Instead of Hate.** Nonviolence resists violence of any form—including "violence of the spirit and violence of the body," and chooses to keep love at the center. "Yes, it is love that will save our world and our civilization, love even for enemies," Dr. King said.
>
> **#6: Peaceful Resistance Believes That the Universe Is on the Side of Justice.** That is, the natural law is on the side of the peaceful, nonviolent resister. This is an act of faith: to know that peaceful nonviolent resistance will eventually win.

Step 6: Sparking Peaceful Revolutions | 93

Serve as Prophetic Witness

Dr. Martin Luther King Jr. taught people in the Civil Rights Movement that each of us has the opportunity to serve as a "prophetic witness" when we embark in peaceful resistance. The four aspects of prophetic witness are listed below, together with questions inspired by them.

Take a moment to journal on the following questions.

What Is My Calling? A calling is about recognizing where our inner compass draws us.

What Are My Convictions? Clarifying our convictions is about touching into our connection with expanded awareness through unify consciousness. It's choosing deliberately in alignment with our "deployment" (see Step 2).

How Can I Be Courageous? In every aspect of life, courage is about being willing to take risks in service to our calling. Another way to tap into courage is to ask: "What am I willing to sacrifice?"

What Are My Commitments? Clarifying and reaffirming our commitments is about sustaining and invigorating our work of service over the long term. My question to you: Will you commit to living as a love-centered activist? And what might that look like?

GROUP DISCUSSION QUESTIONS

1. What arose for you as you explored serving as a prophetic witness?
2. What are your experiences with peaceful, nonviolent resistance?
3. What do you think are the best ways to use peaceful resistance to accomplish your visions?
4. What fears arise for you when you consider participating in peaceful resistance?
5. How does joining together as a group help each person to be more courageous?
6. How can your group build a beloved community to support peaceful resistance?
7. How can your group connect with other groups who are supporting peaceful resistance?

Step 6: Sparking Peaceful Revolutions

Rx #18: Self-Care Tips

There is a fine line between stretching ourselves and pushing ourselves to the breaking point. It can be easy to fall into a pattern of overdoing it. In some community cultures, abusing ourselves or others "for the cause" is silently normalized.

Participating in an action, campaign, or a love-centered revolutionary movement can have a strong emotional effect on us that reverberates for a while. Movements are most successful when they create a culture where self-care is built into every aspect of human relations—with staff, volunteers, and allies. It is essential to create a movement culture where it is safe for each person to prioritize caring for every aspect of themselves—their whole person, including their physical, emotional, intellectual, and spiritual well-being.

Here are some tips that I have found to be extraordinarily helpful.

Self-Care as the #1 Priority

Before, during, and after a direct action, here is a checklist of things you can do to optimize your self-care:

1. **Self-Reflection:** Take time for self-reflection, which will help you to process your emotions and thoughts. Acknowledge and validate your feelings—before, during, and after.

2. **Reach out for support:** Connect with trusted friends, family, or a therapist who can provide emotional support and a listening ear.

3. **Scheduled downtime:** Allocate specific time for self-care activities and relaxation. Whether it's through reading, meditation, spiritual practices, or a favorite hobby, prioritize downtime.

4. **Physical exercise:** Engage in physical activities to release tension and stress. Exercise is a great way to boost your mood and promote overall well-being—in body, mind, and spirit.

5. **Mindfulness and meditation:** Practice mindfulness and meditation techniques to stay present and grounded. These practices can help manage anxiety and stress.

6. **Limit exposure:** Control your exposure to discussions about crises in the world and the trauma that people are experiencing, especially on social media. Take breaks from engaging with related content when needed. Social media and news holidays are highly recommended.

7. **Create a safe space:** Establish a safe and comfortable environment where you can relax and decompress without external pressures. This space can serve you well both when you're in preparation mode and during aftercare.
8. **Celebrate achievements:** Acknowledge and celebrate your courage for sharing your experiences with others. Recognize the strength it takes to participate in direct action.

(Adapted from the Heat Initiative https://protectchildrennotabuse.org)

GROUP DISCUSSION QUESTIONS

1. How do you care for yourself as you work to care for the world? What do you do well, and where do you fall short?
2. What ways do you use self-care practices when you are preparing for an action? During the action? And after the action? (An "action" is anything you're doing to further your cause, such as a be a meeting, presentation, or taking nonviolent direct action.)
3. How can others (perhaps the other members of this group) support you in your self-care?
4. What can you offer others in support of their self-care?
5. What systems need to be in place to ensure that every person in the group prioritizes and practices self-care?
6. Can your group consider ways to support each other in your self-care needs?
7. What experiences did people in the group have when sharing this practice with others?

Rx #19: Failing Forward

Most activists have fallen on their faces many times. Many of the movements that I've been part of have failed. It also took me a long time to realize that these failures were some of the most valuable experiences I have had, offering tremendous learning and growth.

The concept of "failing forward" is using failure as an opportunity to learn in order to do it better next time. We can take lemons and make them into lemon meringue pie. We can transform our inner dragon into our inner angel, who becomes one of our greatest guides.

It's important to welcome failure as an opportunity for learning and growth. Any given outward success can still leave a trail of psychic wounds and burned-out souls. That's not a true success. True success shows that, whatever the outcome, we have created safe spaces, practiced mutual respect, and advocated for self-care. It has taken me a very long time, and finally I've learned that the journey itself is more important than the outcomes and any final destination. It really is all about the journey!

This is hard work. And it's work that we have to do in a holistic way—with ourselves, our families, our communities, and the world. When we have a support system of fellow Revolutionary Optimists, it's far easier to keep hope alive. We're human. We're going to make mistakes. We're going to fail. We're going to be hyper-emotional at times when we want to be calm. When these things happen—which they will—we can experience the failures as teachable moments. *What can I learn here? What can we learn? Is there a healing opportunity? How can this roadblock help me stretch myself or grow?* This is the process of failing forward—this is progress. I have resolved to treat every failure as a stepping stone into a better me and a better future for everyone.

Failing Forward

Grab a journal and do the following practice in a quiet space where you won't be disturbed. You may also do this practice together with a group of people. Before starting, bring a recent project "failure" to mind that you would like to explore.

1. **Press the pause button on shame.** Before going into the shame-induced cycle of despair we're all familiar with, simply pause. Give yourself permission to feel despair later if you want to, but for now resolve to explore the incident with curiosity first.
2. **Ask yourself, what worked well?** Just because you didn't get the outcome you wanted doesn't mean everything that happened was a failure. How was communication (internal and external) over the course of the

experience? Were there moments of engagement from yourself or others? What contacts came out of this endeavor? When were you actually enjoying yourself? When did others seem to be fully engaged? See what there is to be grateful for here.

3. **Ask yourself, what didn't work?** Explore what didn't work as objectively as you can, without judgment or blame. Again, ask questions about each specific area of the project and look at these factors over time. Can you discern when things started to break down, and why? Did you have a gut feeling at some point along the way that you can pay attention to next time? Ask others involved for their perspective on what they'd do differently next time.

4. **Ask yourself about your internal experience.** How have I grown through this experience? Was I following my inner compass? When did I notice myself shrinking or growing? Where am I feeling more confident? How will these lessons benefit me and others in the future? How will they make me a better person and a more effective activist?

5. **Feel gratitude for the experience.** Recognize that the value of the lessons outweighs anything else you could have accomplished.

Group Discussion Questions

1. What is one of your greatest "failures," and what did you learn from it? Where might you be now if you hadn't learned that lesson when you did?
2. How do you ordinarily respond to failure? What is one thing you could do differently that would be more constructive?
3. As each person in the group shares their experience with a failure, what lessons can be learned for future actions?
4. As a group, what did you learn that you may not have ever discovered unless you explored your failures?
5. How can your organization or movement build systems to learn from failures?
6. Can the group consider organizing a fail forward festival with your community or with a movement of movements?
7. What are the benefits and challenges the group experienced when working as a movement-of-movements?

REVOLUTIONARY OPTIMISM
Journal & Workbook

STEP 7
Unifying

STEP 6
Sparking Peaceful Revolutions

STEP 1
It's Go Time!

STEP 5
Imagineering

7 Steps for Living as a Love-Centered Activist

STEP 2
Self-Liberation

STEP 4
Peace-Crafting

STEP 3
Accessing Unify Consciousness

Step 7: Unifying

UNIFYING COLLECTIVELY is about building a safe, trusting space between different people and movements that are operating locally, statewide, or globally. It is also about looking at things in an intersectional way and determining how to bring together people with inter-partisan perspectives—to be willing, in a sense, to look through one another's eyes.

Unifying means opening up to gain allies in unlikely places—even from the opposing side. It may be necessary to apply peace-crafting work, which we covered in Step 4, individually and in movement-building.

Though we may not realize it, we are already part of an ever-evolving global movement of movements. Our individual acts, our campaigns, and our multiple movements appear at first glance to be singular and independent, and when we are unifying we see that we are part of a larger interconnected movement for justice that spans the entire globe.

Unifying also happens inside of ourselves! As we clarify our inner purpose, our work is to align our entire life to be aligned and driven by our inner purpose. Recognizing that our life and every other life is sacred and also remembering that death can come at any moment is a powerful way of clarifying how we want to share our love and spend our time. Lastly, we are ready to consider making commitments to live as a love-centered activist and/or a Revolutionary Optimist.

Rx #20: Looking for Unifying Opportunities

As individuals who are either part of a movement currently or may be in the future, we might derive inspiration by thinking in terms of an ecosystem. Each species in an ecosystem cares for its own needs and unknowingly contributes to the whole. Our diverse movements may each contribute to a greater transformation.

Looking for Unifying Opportunities

Unifying happens any time we remove separation. So let's do a little journaling on ways that we, collectively, can take down the walls that keep us from thriving. Allow your creative imagination to flow without second-guessing yourself, or other forms of self-censorship!

Imagine you are going to have your eyes checked by the eye doctor, and you are asked what you can see when you look through different lenses. Take out your journal and a pen and explore how we could use peace-crafting practices to explore how you or your movement can mobilize, connect, and engage people through all of these different lenses.

Intersectional: How can we explore and advocate for intersectional equity—transformation of systems of inequality based on gender, race, ethnicity, sexual orientation, gender identity, disability, class, and other forms of discrimination?

Interclass: How can we aim for equity between economic classes?

Intersectoral: How can we build movements between sectors (e.g., education, health, agriculture, technology sectors) where weaving forces can spark bold transformation?

Interspiritual: How can we connect and weave together people of faith, across all religions and including non-believers, so all are invited to connect at a humanistic and/or spiritual level?

Interpartisan: How can we connect people across the political spectrum, including inactive eligible voters, to generate solutions that work for all?

Intergenerational: How can we engage and connect all ages in unified action?

Inter-neighborhood: How can we engage and connect with all our neighbors and between neighborhoods?

International: How can we engage and connect with peoples of all nations?

Interpersonal: How can we strengthen our interpersonal relationships with people who may not always agree with us?

Group Discussion Questions

1. Share your experience of the journaling exercise with the group.
2. Which unifying opportunity do you think is the most important to you? What are the top three priorities for your group, organization, or movement?
3. What unifying opportunity is the most challenging for you? What ideas do you or the group have for moving forward to explore the challenges?
4. What experiences have you had where you or a group has failed to address one or more of these unifying opportunities? What lessons can be learned from these failures?
5. How can your organization or movement build systems to consider all of the unifying opportunities over time?
6. Can your group explore creating in-person opportunities to explore unifying in your communities or as a movement-of-movements?
7. What were the opportunities and challenges that emerged when the group was experiencing the practice of unifying?

Step 7: Unifying

Rx #21: Unify Your Vision and Action

We can't expect ourselves to be perfect, but on the other hand, we must each take stock of where we are falling short of living our stated values. The key is to find a healthy balance point—the place where we are living *into* the world we wish to create, while standing firm in our present reality.

You can align with your inner truth too. You don't need to start a podcast, get a degree, or take a job with a nonprofit if you find yourself adrift from your vision. Having those positive feelings of inner unity are all about the daily choices we make. Will you make time to volunteer with an organization you believe in? Will you choose not to shut out the suffering of the world and instead begin to respond, even in a small way? Will you speak truth to power?

My own experience has taught me that it is possible to have alignment with your values, your life vision, and your inner truths. In this exercise, you will explore the alignment of your vision and your action.

Unify Your Vision and Action

Take out your journal and a pen and write on the following questions:

- What is your vision for the world? And how does it align with your core values? If you're unclear about this, revisit Step 5.
- What actions are you taking in alignment with your vision for the world? Consider each of the four circles of service from Step 1: Self, Loved Ones, Community, World.
- What actions are you taking that are *not* in alignment with your vision? Are there actions you know you should take but are not taking? Consider each of the four circles.
- Reflect on your answers to the first three questions, then answer the following:
    > What is one action you feel called to start doing to align with your vision? Make this a small, achievable action that you can follow through on in a timely way.
    > What is one action that you are called to stop doing? Again, make this small enough that you're confident you can follow through on it.

Group Discussion Questions

1. Share your reflections from the journaling exercise with the group.
2. Is your personal life set up to support your being able to live your life's vision?
3. Are your relationships working to support your being able to live your life's vision?
4. Is your job(s) aligned with your values and supporting you to live your life's vision?
5. If you answered "no" to any of the above, how do you handle the inner conflicts or doubts that arise when your life is not aligned with your life's vision?
6. What actions can you take to align your life vision with the way you are living your life?
7. How can the group members support each other to align each persons' life vision with the way they are living their life?

Rx #22: Death Awareness

Recognizing that our life and all life is sacred and precious is an important practice for living as a love-centered activist. Each day I remind myself that my death can come at any moment, so I have the opportunity to live each day as if it is my last day.

This practice is a powerful way of clarifying how we want to share our love and spend our time. We can aim to live each moment, each day, with full awareness—as if it were all that was left.

Death Awareness Practice

Authors Stephen Levine, Richard Carlson, and Kristine Carlson teach us how a death awareness practice can show us how to live each moment, each day, with full awareness—as if it were all that was left. Inspired by their respective bodies of work, here are some questions to explore:

If you knew that you had an hour to live, whom would you call? What would you say? Imagine calling the most beloved people in your life and start writing what you would say to them.

If you knew you had a week to live, what would you do? How would you spend your time? Imagine what you would say and how you would feel if you were meeting with loved ones in person, on Zoom, or in celebration of life events.

If you knew you had a month to live, what would you complete as part of your legacy? Do you have any projects, activities, or actions that you would prioritize getting done?

If you had a year to live, what would you record in a video or write in a letter to those you love the most? Who are the top ten people you want to inspire with a final message?

Whom will you call *today* to tell that you love them? Why wait? Today may be your last day alive. I hope not, but you never know.

GROUP DISCUSSION QUESTIONS

1. Share your reflections from the journaling exercise with the group.
2. What was it like to face your own mortality while doing this practice?
3. What fears arose when you imagined your own death or the death of a loved one?
4. After doing this practice, what actions are you taking to live with death awareness?
5. How can you share your death awareness practice with people that you love in your life?
6. What were your experiences of sharing the death awareness practice with others in your life?
7. Share with the group any experiences and insights using the death awareness practice on a regular basis as part of one's life.

Rx #23: Self-Commitment to Living as a Love-Centered Activist

Many years ago, I decided to live by Yoda's philosophy from the *Star Wars* movies. While training Luke Skywalker to be a Jedi knight, he says: "Do or do not, there is no try." I have worked to eradicate the word "try" from my personal lexicon, in both my speech and written word, as the use of this word allows me to escape from my commitments. Rather, I say that I will do this. Or I won't do this. I will not try. I commit to how I will act without leaving an escape route.

Take a pen and paper and draft your own commitment to living as a Revolutionary Optimist (or whatever new identity you choose). Feel free to create your own list of commitments, or you can make edits and additions to the certificate below. Also, consider sharing your new commitment with a loved one who could serve as witness.

Self-Commitment: I Am a Love-Centered Activist

Many years ago, I decided to live by Yoda's philosophy from the *Star Wars* movies. While training Luke Skywalker to be a Jedi knight, he says: "Do or do not, there is no try." I have worked to eradicate the word "try" from my personal lexicon, in both my speech and written word, as the use of this word allows me to escape from my commitments. Rather, I say that I will do this. Or I won't do this. I will not try. I commit to how I will act without leaving an escape route.

Take a pen and paper and draft your own commitment to living as a Revolutionary Optimist (or whatever new identity you choose). Feel free to create your own list of commitments, or you can make edits and additions to the certificate below. Also, consider sharing your new commitment with a loved one who could serve as witness.

I am committed to the survival and thriving of all of humanity.
I am committed to ensuring that all of humanity has the opportunity to realize happiness.
I am committed to supporting human rights for all.
I will use my life to urgently address the super-crises that humanity is facing.
I see each person as precious and sacred, with unalienable rights to justice, equality, and dignity.
I am committed to living as a love-centered activist.
I am committed to living as a Revolutionary Optimist.

Signature: _____

Date: _____

Witness (optional): _____

Group Discussion Questions

1. Share the commitment you are making with the group.
2. How are your personal commitments linked to addressing the super-crises that we face today?
3. What are your personal commitments to putting love at the center of our social, economic, and political systems?
4. What does it feel like to self-identify as a love-centered activist?
5. What does it feel like to self-identify as a Revolutionary Optimist?
6. Does our group want to continue to meet regularly to ensure that each has support as we live into our Revolutionary Optimism lives?
7. Does our group want to connect with other Revolutionary Optimism groups and #unify?

Journey Onward

DR. MARTIN LUTHER KING JR. spoke to our revolutionary spark during his famous speech titled "Beyond Vietnam: A Time to Break Silence," which he delivered on April 4, 1967, at the Riverside Church in New York City, exactly one year before he was assassinated:

> We are now faced with the fact that tomorrow is today. We are confronted with the fierce urgency of now. In this unfolding conundrum of life and history, there is such a thing as being too late. Procrastination is still the thief of time. Life often leaves us standing bare, naked, and dejected with a lost opportunity. The "tide in the affairs of men" does not remain at the flood; it ebbs. We may cry out desperately for time to pause in her passage, but time is adamant to every plea and rushes on. Over the bleached bones and jumbled residues of numerous civilizations are written the pathetic words, "Too late."

Dr. King's call to action is a powerful reminder to take bold and transformative action in the face of injustice, oppression, and inequality. It serves as a rallying cry for us all to work tirelessly towards creating a more just, equitable, and inclusive society. We are in a moment of human history when our collective action is needed now-now! We are called to rise to meet this moment of despair with courage, compassion, and resilience.

The destructive forces of caste, greed, and thirst for power are waging a violent revolution right now, leaving many people feeling hopeless, despairing, and confused. At the same time, millions of people around the world right now are working steadily and humbly on a peaceful revolution of compassion and justice. And you are one of those people.

For a much deeper dive into Revolutionary Optimism than this workbook can offer, I invite you to read or share a copy of the book that started it all: *Revolutionary Optimism: 7 Steps for Living as a Love-Centered Activist*. In it, you'll find essential background, stories, and frameworks that will accompany you like trusted friends on your journey to change the world.

Now that you have completed the exercises in this workbook, what's next? These tools are designed to be used again and again throughout our lives. Like a well-made hammer or broom, they can be kept handy and taken out again whenever needed.

I recommend choosing one or two tools that especially resonated with you and integrating them into your daily life. You may wish to include them as part of a daily meditation practice or journaling session. Once these have become a habit, feel free to add more. Just don't try to take on too much at once—that is a recipe for quitting altogether.

I also suggest revisiting this workbook in its entirety every so often, ideally with a small group of friends or colleagues. You may be surprised by how your answers and understandings evolve over time.

It has been my greatest honor to accompany you through these pages. I wish you well on your journey to transform yourself and our world.

Our work continues each day and every day of our lives. It's go time!

Acknowledgments

SPECIAL THANKS to Nicholas Tippins for your support in writing and editorial support of this workbook. Gratitude to Chelsea Hamre for the book cover design, to Alex Lubertozzi for the internal book design and editorial support, and for publishing support from Kristine Carlson and Debra Evans of Book Doulas, and Megan Williams and Ira Vergani, The Self-Publishing Agency.

Gratitude to Amber Rose, Brandon Lee, Patti Zorr, and Jackie Lapin for getting *Revolutionary Optimism* out in the world.

I'm deeply grateful for all of my justice-centered advocacy and movement-building colleagues over years, and I'm excited for our onward collaborations. Your bravery and our solidarity fuels and inspires my journey. I am blessed to be surrounded by a love-centered community of spirit buddies.

Gratitude to Mom and late Father for the gift of my life. To my sister, Marci, for your lifelong love. To my beloved wife, Mindi, my journey is enlivened every day by your unconditional love, your wit, and even your skepticism. To my children and grandchildren, being part of your journeys ignites the love spark within me.

About the Author

DR. PAUL ZEITZ is a preventive medicine physician, epidemiologist, author, and award-winning champion of global justice and human rights. Drawing from over thirty-five years of advocacy, campaigning, and political movement leadership, Zeitz is the initiator of #unify Movements, a movement-building platform dedicated to catalyzing new, love-centered social, economic, and political systems committed for our collective repair, justice, and peace. As a new movement, #unifyUSA was launched in 2023 as a peaceful revolutionary political movement to cocreate a United States 2.0 through urgent constitutional renewal.

Zeitz has a breadth of experience spanning diverse sectors including climate transformation, racial and gender equity, authentic democracy, sustainable development, child welfare and global health in the U.S. and globally. Currently, he serves as a co-convenor of the U.S. National Truth, Racial Healing, and Transformation (TRHT) Movement, on the Steering Committee of the March for Equity, and on the Board of Directors of ALEPH: Alliance for Jewish Renewal. Zeitz proudly serves on the Survivor's Council of the Heat Initiative which is dedicated to eradicating childhood sexual violence. His debut memoir published in 2018, *Waging Justice: A Doctor's Journey to Speak Truth and Be Bold*, offers profound personal perspectives on how one's deep individual healing is intricately connected with the repair of our broken world.

As a movement builder during 2000 2023 he cofounded the Brave Movement, Keep Kids Safe, Global Action for Children and the Global AIDS Alliance. During 2015–18, Zeitz worked as the Director, Data Revolution for Sustainable Development, in the Office of the Global AIDS Coordinator, President's Emergency Plan for AIDS Relief (PEPFAR), U.S. Department of State, under both the Obama and Trump administrations. During 1994–2000, Zeitz served in the U.S. Agency for International Development (USAID) in Washington, D.C. and then in Zambia. During 1992–94, he served in the Epidemic Intelligence Service of the Commissioned Corps of the U.S. Public Health Service at the Centers for Disease Prevention and Control (CDC).

Zeitz was ordained as a Shir Hashirim (Song of Songs) Rabbi in 2023. He has been certified by the American Board of Preventive Medicine since 1993. Married for over 32 years, Paul and his wife, Mindi, are the proud parents and grandparents of Birdie, Cletus, Emet, Erica, Korra, Lian, Rikki, Skye Joy, Sunny, Uriel, and Yonah.

Made in United States
Troutdale, OR
06/15/2025